Strangely Marked Metal

STRANGELY MARKED METAL

poems by
Kay Ryan

Copper Beech Press

Some of these poems originally appeared in *International Poetry Review*, *Mendocino Review*, *Ohio Journal*, *Pacific Review*, *PN Review*, and *Poetry* ("The Egyptians" and "Marianne Moore Announces Lunch," copyright© 1984 by the Modern Poetry Association).

The publication of this book was made possible by a grant from the National Endowment for the Arts, a Federal agency, in Washington, D.C.

For information, address the publisher:
Copper Beech Press
Post Office Box 2578
Providence, Rhode Island 02906

Library of Congress Cataloging in Publication Data
Ryan, Kay.
Strangely marked metal.

I. Title.
PS3568.Y38S8   1985   811'.54   85-11372
ISBN 0-914278-46-0 (alk. paper)

Second Printing
Printed in the United States of America

for Carol

CONTENTS

Strangely Marked Metal

Like boulders rolled away from doors,
like meteors, things rumbling
in my brain ask me
to go like Moses out
into some wilderness.

I have no people.
I have no faith.
I am not among the fortunate
banished forever
from the sweet named waters
of their own land, who can
roam the earth's face relying
on the pain of resemblance; I
mistake no crevice in you, earth,
for some dear place lost.

I have no people.
I have no faith.
I do not hear voices that can
tell me what to do if I am
fearless. The boulders are
faceless, anonymous, everything
but soundless.

Bring me to my people
Bring me to my place.
Let me watch the waters
close at the last act
of the miracle; let me be
delivered among the lost, equally
lost, and thankful to one
another that we are not
more cruel.
Let me visit my past like

stations of the cross,
let me feel the
ritual words, each
stumble, each kiss,
at least betrayal — let me know this.

What is as delightful
as a palpable silence,
a creamy latex of a
silence, stirrable
with a long stick. Such
a silence is particularly
thick at the bottom, a
very smooth lotion, like
good paint by the gallon.
This is a base silence,
colored only by addition,
say a small squeeze of
green when the bird sings
idly of trees he has
seen. It is a clean
silence, the kind that
does not divide us,
like dreams it is
viscous but like good dreams
where sweet things last and
last past credibility.
Even in the dream we know
it is a luxury.

It waits in the ear
perhaps no more
than a balance problem
like the chip in a gear
that causes a brief
rest in motion.
But when silence blooms
it says *forever.*
There was never a time
that was not this flower.
It waits in the ear
as death or angels. It
can possess the Earth
a sudden shadow
or endless absence
of shadow. If you could
walk over to those trees
there would be no shade
under them and no breeze.
Or if there were a breeze
it would say *hair* or *skin.*
It would not say *you;* it
could not get in.

THE ADMIRABLE BEDE, 7TH-CENTURY ENGLISH HISTORIAN

It is good for history to be told; the acts of the virtuous will
encourage virtue, and evil will warn against evil.

There has always been a Machiavelli, urban
and lettered, who will find in all ancient wisdom
the pattern of human vulnerability; he will be
brilliant; his reason will shine like mail,
each silver scale fitted cunningly
over the last. His cruel understanding will
seem to prevail for a long time; he will prove
that man can never arm himself against himself
thoroughly enough, that he is a jointed creature
strung haphazardly, an easy puppet to any strong hand;
a look at the land shows the welts of walls
and earth works meant to stand against Pict, Saxon,
Angle, heathen and Christian. Saints sizzle
like all bacon. Every century and fraction
of century is disheartened; part of every home
and monastery is turned against itself;
each man has something withered
or a misplaced tooth or an eye that wanders;
each soul its own barbarian bent on plunder —
call it Machiavelli; give him history,
let him march through the city,
let him name the streets and currency, let
everyone bow down before his own worst possibility
manifest; there will be the other part of the city —
like the flower which thrives on neglect, or
the grace by which monuments slide down to stacks
upon which some shepherd sits, half loving,
half hating his life, drawing his flute
out of his sleeve, one eye on the clouds
one eye on the sheep.

Always and always
it has been so —
the wave that has foamed
on the sand
must swell and
come in again
and again while
you are sleeping
and again when you are
on the dry desert.
This wave must forever
reform and foam
and forever
there will be
two women
lying easily
on cushions,
the weather
will be warm.
Her arm
will lie across
her brow, palm
slightly open;
her friend will
lean down.
They will talk
of nothing
of importance,
an easy voluptuousness,
a soft wash
of light on garments.
Their limbs
may intertwine,
a leg slide
on a leg

from time to time,
like foam on sand —
a thing of no consequence.
There is nothing
to endurance.
It is not a talent.
You or I will
never understand it.

Heavens need furnaces,
the factories where dross
converts to light gasses.
The sloughed skins of dreams
are instant fuel, remarkably
full of oil like creosote
bushes. Your worst losses
warm angels; despair puts
a glint on God's hair. And
the nicest surprise is
the substance that rises
when you know you can't
get there from here.

"IN THE VERY ESSENCE OF POETRY
THERE IS SOMETHING INDECENT"

After a brief period
during youth who among us
would not prefer to say yes,
would not work with a will
to raise high the roofbeam
of a good house? Who
if they could choose
would not gladly trade
words for wood, and feel
through the hammer's shaft
the plant cells weld
around the nail? Who would
whisper *death,* and *death?*
There are poets whose names
alone bring pain, and
single poems that drain
more than anyone wanted
to hold, or burn up hope
for fuel. Who would have
what they say end before
the wheel swings up again?
It is cruel comfort to
insist that the arc is
part of a circle, by will
remember the hand
touches others, to swear
the word finds a home
and grows young again
and fickle.

Hope should come to a full stop.
My vision is gone, gone! Ariadne
on the shore; Theseus went on
in his ship, tapped by his own fate.
She stands, her silk garments paint
her ankles, her grief is marble.
Maybe she will find something later,
some laughter like flame,
but she stands now queen
of all her pain, commanding the
demesne of her curse, no half
kiss on her lips. She was
fast asleep when he left; the place
where his sail slipped over
the edge of the earth is open in her;
her bed keeps no false warmth.

The new ascetics
have the desert rabbit
as their totem object.
They admire his ears
scooped to clear
tympanies from base to tip,
flared like spoons and smooth
and hairless, tuned to an
infinite array of enemies.
The ascetics like his dignity.
Yes his ears swivel independently
as he nibbles some green.
There are more things
to be afraid of
than anyone has seen.

GAMBLER

He's seen all he can of moon,
the white which names black;
he's had enough of that.
There is no randomness behind
the card's face; the night
waits to erase change, each trace.

Why is china not shamed in the presence
of the bull? Should it not shatter of
its own failure, spontaneously sunder
its fragile understanding of proper behavior,
grind back to sand, working its frail handles
like cricket legs to say, "Relieve us
from careful hands. If we are avatars
it is of enduring hunger. Let us
in the presence of the raking bull
return to pinched imitations of gourds
and shells, the first impulse to hold
what won't be held. Let our closeness
to uses be our elegant translucence."

I do not mind belonging to
a dying vision.
I do not mind if the blue
color will not mean the virgin,
if the song of the shepherd's
crook is forgotten. It is delight
like last light making the
longest pattern. It is sweet
like the earned night. There
must be rest. Let the old
beauty sleep in the monastery
that always keeps the boundary
of the nearly forgotten —
quiet, unable to help the
resurrection. It is wrong to
invite barbarians, who will
on their own be too enamoured
of the old wisdom. Cast upon
cast will be taken of the
saved forms after the first
destruction and alarm. All
this will be born again, and
by grace of ignorance
catch the first light from
the opposite horizon.

THE BARBARIAN'S REPLY

I am the barbarian
no one may call,
currently thought
to dwell within
the silicon circuitries
of your crude machinery.
This is not the case
at all.

You cannot invent me.
It is always the West
and I always
went thataway.
Know me by my damage,
the dear wreckage
you desire to restore.
You know what I mean.
I can say no more.

She envied the mathematical eye of a bird
and its beak which made some sticks
hopeless to its purpose. The forest,
she suspected, is nearly electric
to a nesting bird. Right twigs blaze red
as the parts of the Bible Jesus said. There is
an economical motion in a bird's arrival
on a limb which will serve as arch
or atrium to the next generation.
They know how large their babies will be,
she thought, and build accordingly.

Where were the tablets before Moses?
Were they folded like the wings of an insect
hidden deep in soft earth?
Or were they undistinguished igneous,
part of a black blanket of volcanic efflatus?
Did the law or did it not exist
to be retrieved as needed or was it
created on the spot, as Vesuvius
defined a way of life: Pompeii's
wine shops shall forever have this
owner and this drunkard; this husband
shall bed between this wife and servant.
Children shall no longer be random and
birds shall be cinders. Oh birds shall
be cinders and dogs shall curl like
shrimps; trees shall be veins in stone;
there shall not be leaves. A terrible
shoe that fits, the law of Vesuvius.
But what if the tablets are shrapnel,
working their way in the soil, and Moses
on hand when some surfaced?
Is this ridiculous? Perhaps
they are all the sáme strangely marked metal
which we cannot resist reading as fiercely
as we can because they are so beautiful.

TO THE VIETNAMESE BOY HOUNDED AND AT LAST MURDERED BY A FELLOW STUDENT AT DAVIS HIGH SCHOOL, MAY 1983

No more than the delicate springbok
were you a saint trimmed to leap
straight up into a moving stasis;
you would graze in ordinary places
and enjoy small successes.
If your jump when wounded
was elegant, it was not
to heat the hunter to pursuit.
You were too badly hurt to tease;
it was only to survive if you
stole lightly back behind his eyes.

FISHING

You can taste it in fish
caught one by one and
brought home from the pond
or river or whatever corner
of water offers. The deep
fanned meander, the silver
well and dimple that nets
would plunder. An
almost drowning patience,
a wish so subtle,
so much a thing of flesh
that change and choice mesh —
the bright barbed hook as strange
to fisherman as fish. How odd
to be caught or to catch; something
of this stays in the flesh.

DESERT LAKE

Any time after April
the air can grow hot
and compress to the shape
of a lens or a lentil, scraped
on top by a pressure of coolness,
a new lake ripples on the desert's stillness.
It bulges with mirage fishes
swimming among the creosote bushes,
it pulses with salty creatures
desert children only otherwise
see in pictures.

A JAR ALLEGED TO CONTAIN THE ORIGINAL EGYPTIAN DARKNESS INFLICTED BY MOSES

What would anyone do
with such a little bit?
Darkness gets
just so dark
then it quits.

If they let it out
it would be the same
as with Pandora's Box.
Creatures and monsters
could only remind her
of the uselessness
of containers.

They wandered
into corners and bogs
slithered under leaves
and into logs
and made the ugly squeals
which are their delight
at finding their brother
there already and a kindred night.

Novelty had not yet
replaced seasons in
the ancient pantheon
of the Egyptians. With
the available majesty
of the Nile rising
up the legs of the ibis
and flooding the fields
of papyrus, why court
oddity?

                There was
active distaste among
even maize slaves and
stone masons for changes
other than the seasons.
Take Death: too sudden;
thus steps taken such as
the preparations of
Tutankhamen. No Egyptian
liked surprises or the
vagaries of hope, knowing
the water one crosses
shapes to the boat.

Oh the brave and confident,
the habitual people of Egypt
who filled Heaven with Earth
by the cubit.

BYZANTIUM

What boxes they
fashioned for the
least splinter of
Christ's Passion —
crosses and casques
encrusted with
green stones and amethyst —
was there once a child Pope
who wanted to open one up?

A beaker of wine
measured by the
strictest standards
can tell us nothing
of the thirsts
of our predecessors.
Look neither to the
style of the container.
City Greeks drank
from a shallow dish,
soldiers from a
flask of horn,
peasants from a bladder.

To plumb the matter,
refill any dish
until your wish
to think reduces
to a stubbornness
toward beauty:
when all debate
concerns a pouting lip,
the way a fabric drapes,
you take the measure
of antiquity.

ERIK SATIE

*Only that which does
not teach, does not
cry out, does not
persuade, does not
condescend, does not
explain, is
irresistible.* Thus
must we love your
music *du meuble.* Yes
your *longueurs* are
loungeable, your *soussouirs*
rearrangeable to suit
a walk-up flat or suite,
your *coeur* screws into
any lamp, your small fits
enliven long halls
or brighten stairwells, your
songs go anywhere a chair will.
Your passions in the whimsical
colors of cushions please cats
and Persians. Your endless
sadness unrolls before the
tread of Duke or Princess.
From the least distance
your motifs refresh a place,
knots you gave your eyes to
are a saraband of lace.

A brittle
little footsome
crust of jetsam
are the people
from a distance,
a lacy border
to the water.

Oh a girl
is stolen
back to flotsam!

But the mother
goes and
gets her.

Oh the lazy father
fat Poseidon
jams his trident
in the sand
beside him.

And the dog
digs through
to China,
laps jade water,
fights a
gryphon.

As in a dream where I can
never finish packing
I feel the tug of my land
waiting. As though it expects
me to tell it something I know,
something I already
know — and it is so slow, this
packing, this insistence on socks
matching and the intrusion of
other dreams.

BRAVE ROW

Brave row of red yellow and purple soldiers!
Your medals falling from your chests
your epaulets from your shoulders;
all external honors shall be stripped
mercilessly from you as though you were
merely trees and it were merely autumn
and this merely a small song and not an
heroic anthem.

SHRIMP

A shrimp is
almost all antennae.
She conducts the
symphonies.
A whole sea pulses
con anemonae
at her delicate
direction. She
draws the tides
and the slave moon
wanes or fattens.

"WITHOUT MINUTE NEATNESS OF EXECUTION THE SUBLIME CANNOT EXIST!"

And how in this welter
of pigeons, amid this wealth
of feathered diapasons, this
weather of wonder, does the
sublime master disorder? Every
square is a park with shoppers
on their way somewhere, each
still thing statuary, each thought
a law inviting corollaries. Is life
not contrived to bewilder, to abash
by abundance; are there those
among us capable of neatness?
Is it gift or achievement? With a
great rattle the pigeon settles
her feathers, dense now and implacable
as marble she divides the world
into crumbs and pebbles.
With a divine eye she names the edible,
devours it and thus damns each Gretel
(proud of preparations) to the
witch's conflagration. What
could be more sublime than
conjoining bread with belly?
Minute neatness is to pounce
on opportunity.

APPLICATION

Let me be through
with this patience.
I invite crotchets,
I invite the lumpy
pockets of those
firmly established
in their rounds of
debris boxes and
rewarding corners where
the wind delivers lost
lists and bright wrappers.
I apply for a rubber-wheeled
silver Safeway Clipper and
the bone chatter that
stutters up the arms as
it negotiates a gutter.
I apply to the Sisters
of the Doorways. I pledge
not to romanticize our
life together. We are
miserable in bad weather.
But when the sun
shines and a new bank
opens — we warm and strut
innocent as ravens at
the cuffs of alien
celebrations!

TOULOUSE-LAUTREC

Monsieur Lautrec gave his son
a book — *The Art of Falconry* —
writing in it that
when the trials of life
became too wearying
there was comfort
in the company of horses
dogs and falcons (the
script is jumpy — written
in the brougham of some
fancy Madam).

The boy was young and sturdy;
his mother said his presence
filled the house like twenty.
He promised to be
a handsome dallier
like his father
who went out with the
falcons in the night.

This was before the bone disease,
the years in bed,
and long before the dance halls
and the Moulin Rouge,
Lautrec in the forest
of the fancy ladies' legs,
catching them kicked
shoulder-high, legs
that pulled the dancing girls
along and

far up above
as though
in the sky

sharp faces
small and distant
and alone

like falcons.

The sublime is now
a less popular topic
than if El Greco was myopic.
Yes El Greco may very well
have been, which may very
well have made his men
so thin and his women so
distressed. If pressed,
the oculists confess that
the shape taken by the
aqueous humor makes
or breaks us, and have
devised anti-vision devices
that restore noses to their
right lengths and places.
Witness how a speckled plain
condenses to a field
or farmyard, the ecstasy
or pain of space
erased by moving the lens
back or forward.
We now discover there were
many thin kings and
many chubby martyrs,
many ordinary trees
and water always very
similar to our water.

Only a new truth
can bring us closer
to our innocence.
Beyond some point
the sun can't
sweeten old growth.
Last year's oranges
grow giant with rind.

Or consider the
rack of the red deer
when rut is nearly
over: the great structures
break off one at a time

leaving the tired beast
laughably asymmetrical —
our hero who rammed
anything for joy — shy
and bewildered by
his head's odd angle.

Radiant particulars
require a god of mesh.
The eye on this sparrow
must forget itself,
bone, blood and flesh,
yesterday and tomorrow;
give over as the Magi.
Myrrh, frankincense
and golden coffers,
all tribute they had
meant to offer — distant
as the signal star
now watched by shepherds
from afar, beside which
all their guide lights fade.
Oh, god keep what keeps us
unafraid.

With several well-placed
cracks on crystal
she sounds her
somewhat minatory
call to a long (interminable)
light lunch featuring
things barely edible
selected and arranged
for single virtues
such as crunch or
a green translucence.
Celery figures
centrally (though
too complex);
if only the strings
might be plucked
or aeolian we might
achieve Style — a
clarified butter
rather than the
opaque margarine
which spreads of its
own accord, greasing
the jowls of the coarser
gluttons, so common
at any public board
such as this trafficking
in words. The problem
remains how to make
wits rise to a new
level; perhaps
some subtle device
which will secretly
raise the legs of the table?

Unbuild the
Brooklyn Bridge
unspan the river
return travel to water
re-enter a time sunk
in its borders
unthink architect,
steel, stone, send
the laborers home
tired by what they understand
they do not understand.
Let man build
things too steep to climb,
uncrossable, in no way useful,
the butt of the jokes of the
practical. Babel is kinder
than this reminder, this
harp on the way to work,
man-built.

They had been taken far
from their natural homes
on cruel arks, two by two.
They learned odd arts,
to balance balls, sit on stools
and accept food. The food
was the hardest trick, after
the first hunger. They did not
want to strengthen into
this wrong life. Sometimes
they remembered, and
refused to eat. This
saddened their trainer
who had spun all his own wildness
into patience. There must be
great humility in dominance.
One day the elephants
left, still draped in cloth
of sequins, single file, trunk
intertwined with tail, in their
usual sequence. Then the bears,
dogs and big cats drifted off.
There had been a kind of balance
but when the elephants left
it did not make sense not to
bite the hand that fed you.
In fact it was the only
sensible thing to do.
The animals all found
some kind of nature to which
they adapted, like all immigrants.
The only one who could not adjust
was the trainer, who had
conquered too much in himself.

THE SHOW

There will be a show
sometime of the trees
outside the poets' windows,
brought together from Provence,
the Lake District and Chicago.
They will be framed so
that you will see as the poet did.
Some parts will be hidden —
the trunk, or the topmost netting
where the lightest life would be sitting.
It will be worthwhile seeing this;
you will begin to understand what a realist
the strangest poet is. Later when you see his
photograph you will sense the very branches
that wrapped his chest as he sat
where he must have had to sit.
And his manuscript, you will later note,
lacks just such upward or downward strokes
as did his view. You will admire
what a literal thing we have to do.